A FEELING WITHIN

KEVIN PEAY AND JOEL McCAUSLAND

AFTERGLOW

Arrangements by
Greg Hansen

Deseret Book Company
Salt Lake City, Utah

ISBN 0-87579-133-6

Printed in the United States of America

10 9 8 7 6 5 4

CONTENTS

HOLD ON TO LIFE

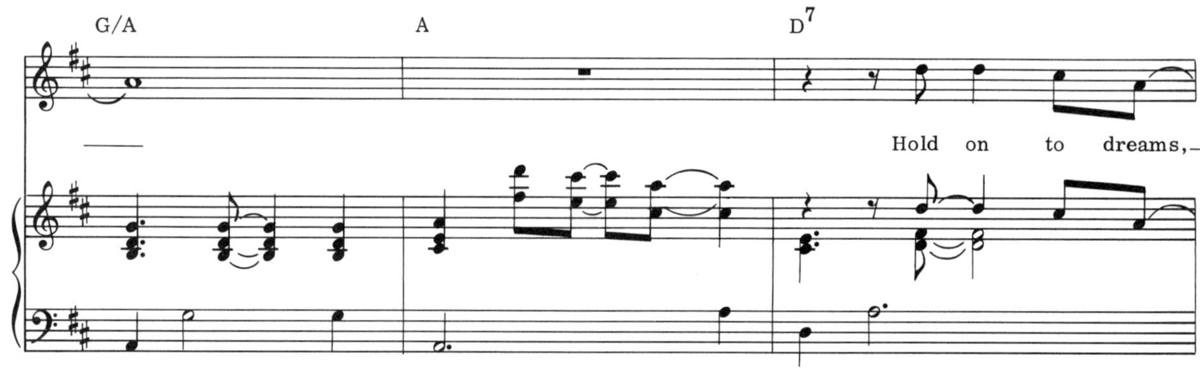
G/A
A
D7
Hold on to dreams,

Bm 7
They may be an - swers to things,

Gma7
G/A
Things that are on your mind.

A/B
D7
Hold on to the pro - mise.

Gma7
G/A
Hold on to the prize; And make ev-'ry day an
G/A
Dadd 9
eas - i - er way By liv - ing your life.
Dadd 9
Gma7
There may be a tri - al, A heart-ache or two some-time,
G/A
But to - day is the bright - er to - mor - row; Start

D add 9
To ⊕ D
liv - ing your life.
espr.

Bm7
Gma7
Em7
Em7/D

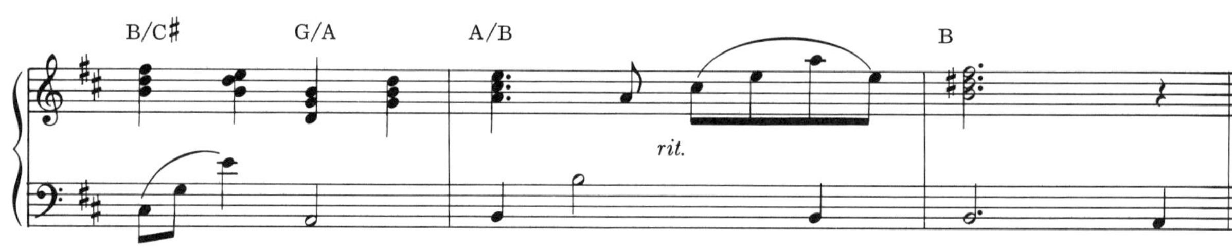
B/C♯
G/A
A/B
B
rit.

D add 9
a tempo
Bm7
Hold on to life.
Al-though it's not ea -
a tempo

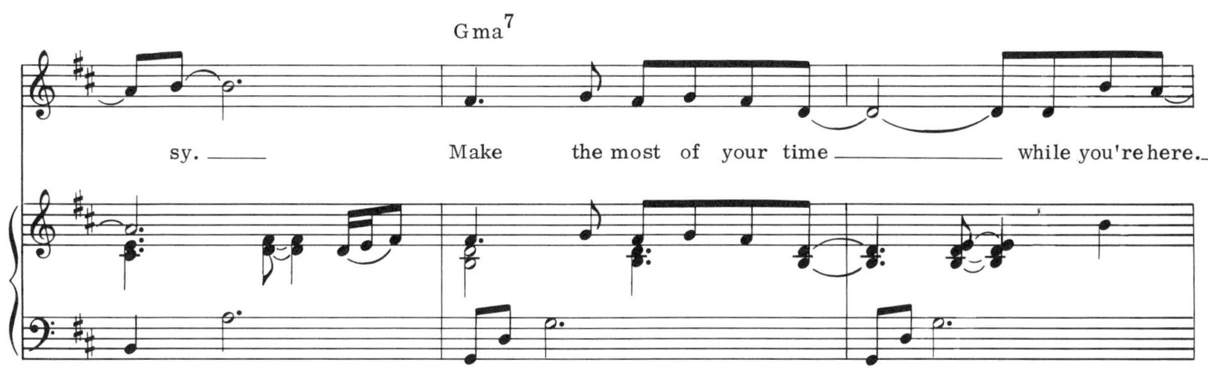
Gma7
sy. Make the most of your time while you're here.

G/A
A
Dadd 9
Hold on to life,

Bm7
'Cause with ev - 'ry mo - ment There lies

Gma7
G/A
A/B
Em/A
Some-one who's hold - ing you near.
D.S. al Coda
D.S. al Coda

Coda
Dadd9
Bm7
Hold on to life,
Hold on to life,
Gma7
Hold on to life,
Hold
G/A
A
Dadd9
Bm7
on
to life.
Gma7
A
A/B
B
rit.

CAPTAIN OF MY SOUL

Arranged by
Greg Hansen

Words and Music by
AFTERGLOW

Slow Ballad

F add 9 C/E Dm7 Dm/C B♭

B♭/C C7 F add 9 C/E Dm7 Dm/C

At times my life is dark__ and so con-fus - ing.__ At

B♭ B♭/C C7 F add 9

times my heart__ is weight - ed with des - pair, 'Cause

F add 9 C/E Dm7 Dm/C

though I try to win,_ seems I'm still los - ing,____ As

B♭
B♭/C
C7
all my ef - forts van - ish in the air. They

F add 9
C/E
Dm7
Dm/C
say you've got - ta fight to gain the glo - ry. They

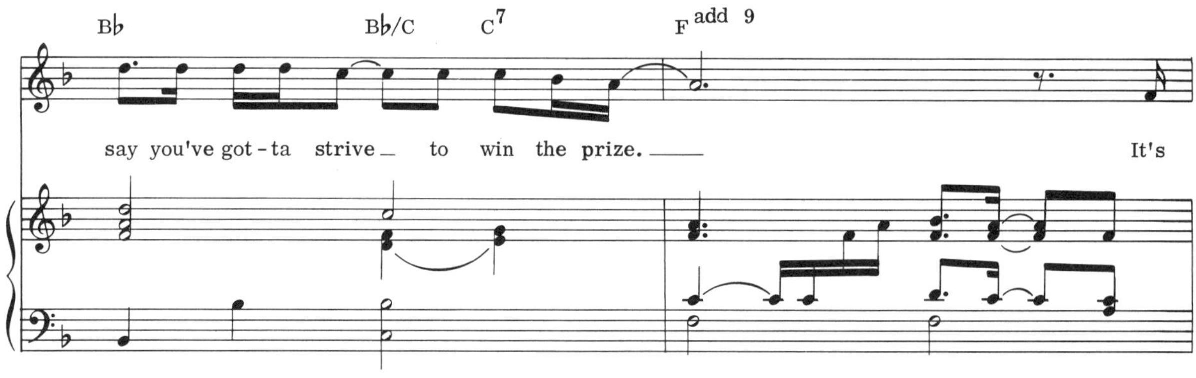
B♭
B♭/C
C7
F add 9
say you've got - ta strive to win the prize. It's

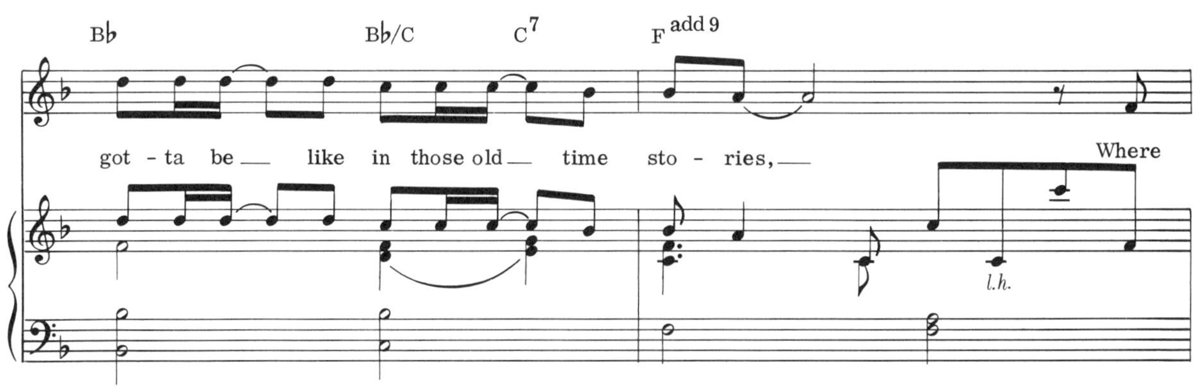
B♭
B♭/C
C7
F add 9
got - ta be like in those old time sto - ries, Where
l.h.

B♭
C sus
F
B♭
B♭/C
he - roes walked with vic-t'ry in their eyes. I am the cap - tain, cap-tain of my
cap - tain, cap-tain of my
f
F
F/A
B♭
B♭/D
B♭/C
C7
soul. Mas - ter of my des - ti - ny. With the
soul. Mas - ter of my des - ti - ny. Know-ing
F
C/E
Dm7
F/C
B♭
truths that I've been giv - en I can choose the path for me. I'm the
end - ing from be - gin - ning, He can plan my course for me. He's the
F
B♭/C
C7
To F add 9
C/E
Dm7
Dm/C
mas - ter of my des - ti - ny.
mas - ter of my des - ti - ny.

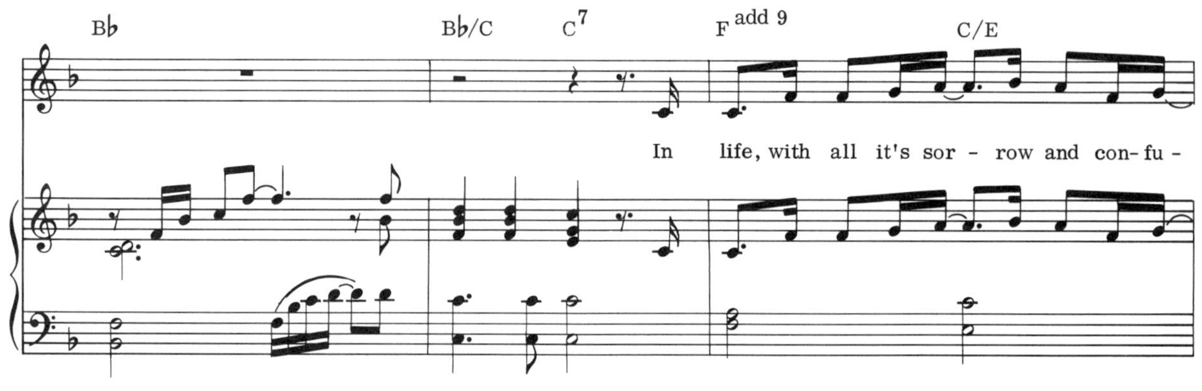
B♭
B♭/C
C7
F add 9
C/E
In life, with all it's sor - row and con- fu -

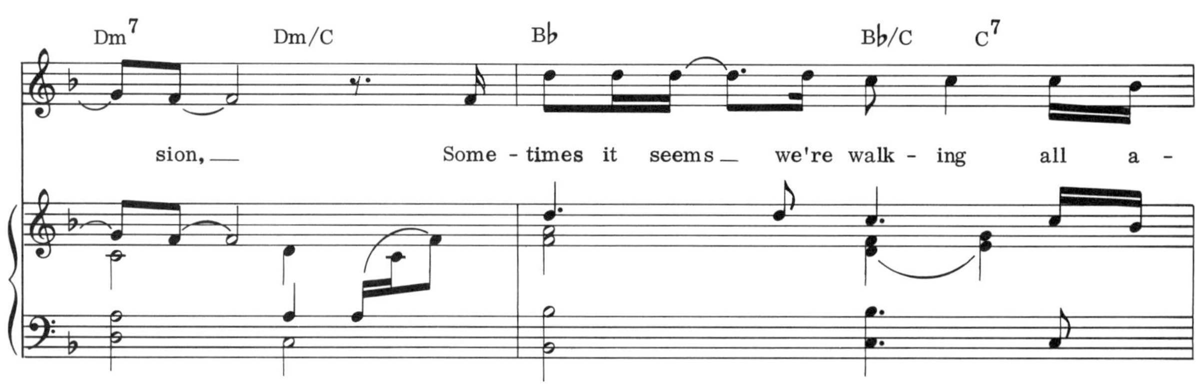
Dm7
Dm/C
B♭
B♭/C
C7
sion, Some - times it seems we're walk - ing all a -

F add 9
F add 9
C/E
lone. There's got - ta be some-one we can re - ly

Dm7
Dm/C
B♭
B♭/C
C7
on. I know we'll nev - er make it on our own. They

F add 9
C/E
Dm7
Dm/C
say you've got - ta fight to gain the glo - ry.
They
B♭
B♭/C
C7
F add 9
say you've got - ta strive to win the prize.
But
B♭
B♭/C
C7
F add 9
one whose name I've heard in Bi - ble sto - ries,
Stands
B♭
B♭/C
C7
wait - ing there with vic - t'ry in His eyes.
He'll be the
D.S. al Coda
D.S. al Coda

Coda
F Bb Bb/C F F/A
cap - tain
ny. Cap - tain of my soul.
f
Bb Bb/D Bb/C C7
Mas - ter of my des - ti - ny. Know - ing
F C/E Dm7 F/C Bb
end - ing from be - gin - ning, He can plan my course for me. He's the
F Bb/C C7 F
mas - ter of my des - ti - ny.

I KNOW HE'S THERE

Arranged by
Greg Hansen

Words and Music by
AFTERGLOW

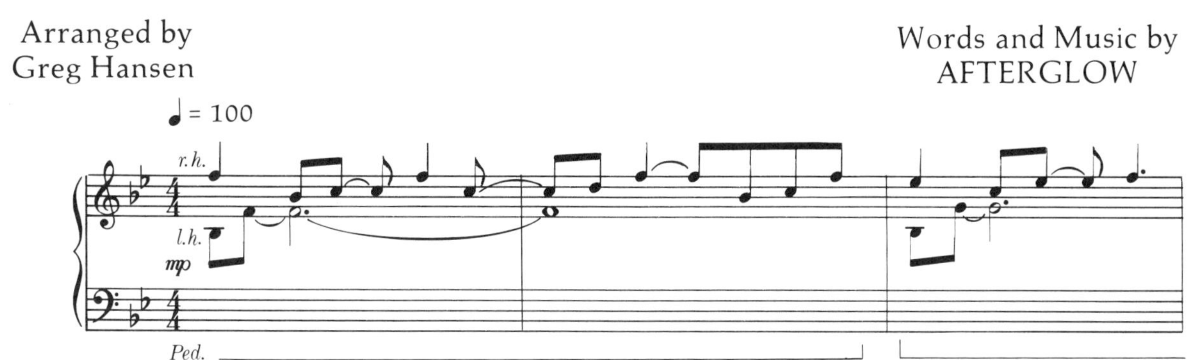

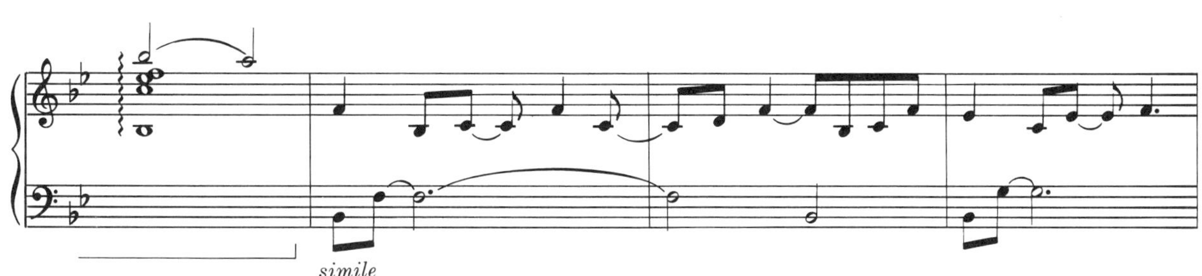

B♭
B♭ add 9 sus 4
B♭
in the air.
When-ev-er I
Gm7
A♭ma9
feel the warmth of the sun in sum - mer,
Or the
B♭
B♭ add 9 sus 4
change of the au - tumn leaves ly - ing there.
E♭add 9
E♭/C
F7
B♭add 9
I know there's some - one who cre - a - ted all I

B♭ma7
E♭ add 9
E♭/F
F7
see, And I sense a qui - et won - der as I try
B♭ add 9
B♭ add 9 sus 4
B♭
to just be - lieve. I feel the rain,
Gm7
A♭ma7
and soon there be - comes a rain - bow, As the
B♭
Gm7
A♭ma7
clouds spell out His name, some - one's there.

A♭ma7
(F7)
f
B♭
B♭ma7
For who made the moun - tains stand and
f
E♭
E♭/F
F
B♭
who made the o - cean shores? And who made you
B♭ma7
E♭
E♭/F
To ⊕
dim.
and I? It's all for a rea - son. Be - lieve that there is a God.
dim.
B♭
r.h.
l.h.
mp

B♭
B♭
Some peo - ple tell me there's
E♭/B♭
B♭
no one there.
But deep in - side
E♭/B♭
I know He lives.
B♭
E♭/B♭
I look a - round me and see what's here,

B♭
Ev - 'ry - thing tells me there is a God.
E♭/B♭
D.S. al Coda
D.S. al Coda
Coda B♭
F/G
C
Cma7
For who made the moun - tains stand, and
F
F/G
G
C
who made the o - cean shore? And who made you

Cma7
F
F/G
f
3
and I? It's all for a rea - son. Be - lieve that there is a

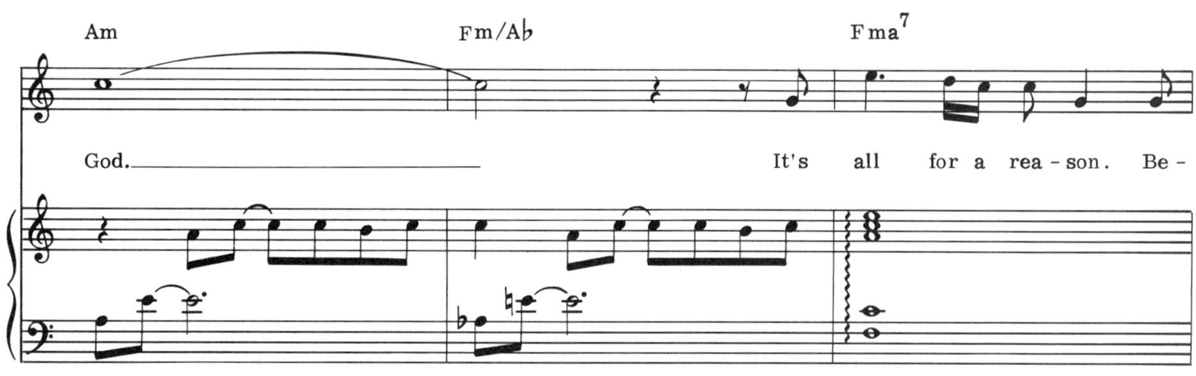
Am
Fm/A♭
Fma7
God. It's all for a rea - son. Be -

F/G
C
3
dim.
lieve that there is a God.
mp

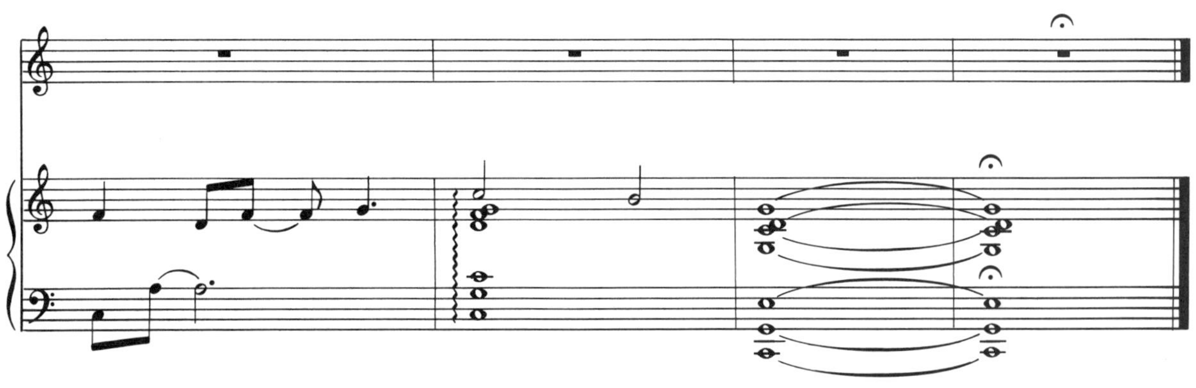

IF ONLY

Arranged by
Greg Hansen

Words and Music by
AFTERGLOW

Rubato - with feeling

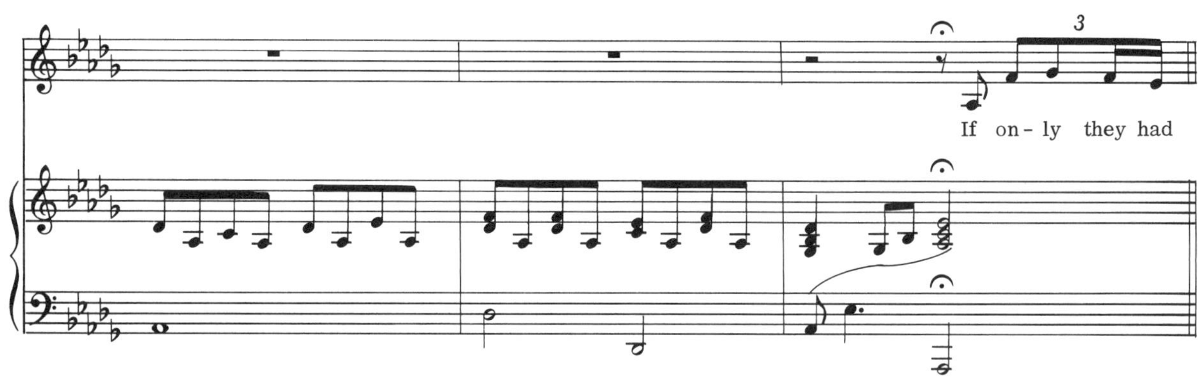

Db Fm7 Gbma7 Gb/Ab Ab7
looked in - to His eyes to un - der - stand what sort of man. If on - ly they had
lis - tened to the words He spoke, the great - est of all time. If on - ly they had
things I've done, at times it seems He sac - ri - ficed in vain. If on - ly I could
Db Fm7 Gbma7 Gb/Ab Ab7 To 1. Db
seen. If on - ly they had known.
heard. If on - ly they had
feel. If on - ly I could
Gb/Ab Ab7 2. Db add 9 Ab/Db Db/F Gbma7 Gb/Ab Ab
If on - ly they had known. Had I been there could I
f
Fm7 Bbm7 Gbma7 Gb/Ab Ab7
stem the tide. Could I stand my ground and hold on 'til the

Db Db7 Gbma7 Gb/Ab Ab7
end? Or in my weak - ness would I
Db Ab/C Bbm7 Gbma7 Ab/Gb Gb
fail the test? Would I show my faith and prove my - self a
Gb/Ab Ab7
friend? If on - ly I could
D.S. al Coda
Coda
Db add 9 Ab/Db Dbma7 Gb G/A Cm7/A
know. If on-ly I could
mf

D
F#m
Gma7
show
The grat - i - tude I
ten.
G/A
A7
G/A
A7
feel in - side,
de - spite my weak - ness,
cresc.
D
F#m7
Gma7
3
G/A
A
f
Ev - 'ry time I try to change His
love can't be de - nied, It's hid-den in my
f
D
Dma7/F#
F#m7
Gma7
A7
heart.
It's writ - ten in my

F♯m7
Bm7
rit.
3
soul.
Want to share it with you
Slower
Gma7
G/A
A7
3
now,
If on - ly you could
D add 9
Bm7
know.
Gma7
G/A
D
rit.

WARRIORS OF LIGHT

Arranged by
Greg Hansen

Words and Music by
AFTERGLOW

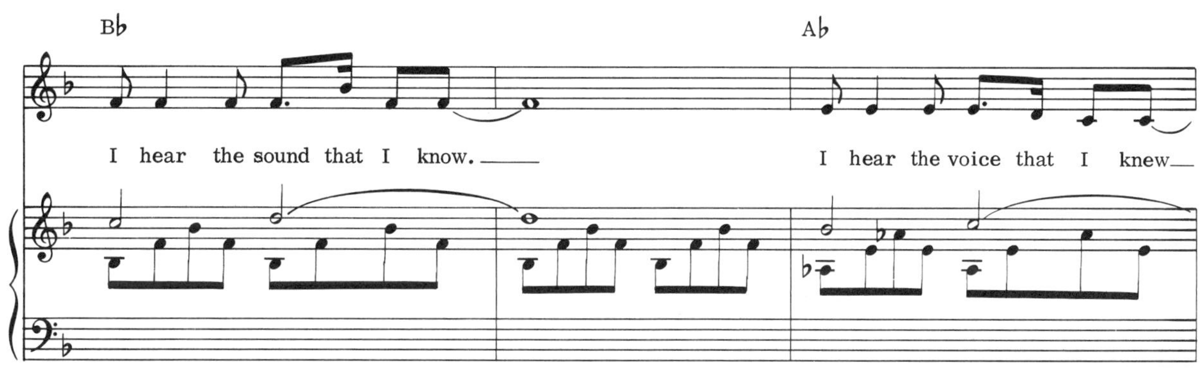

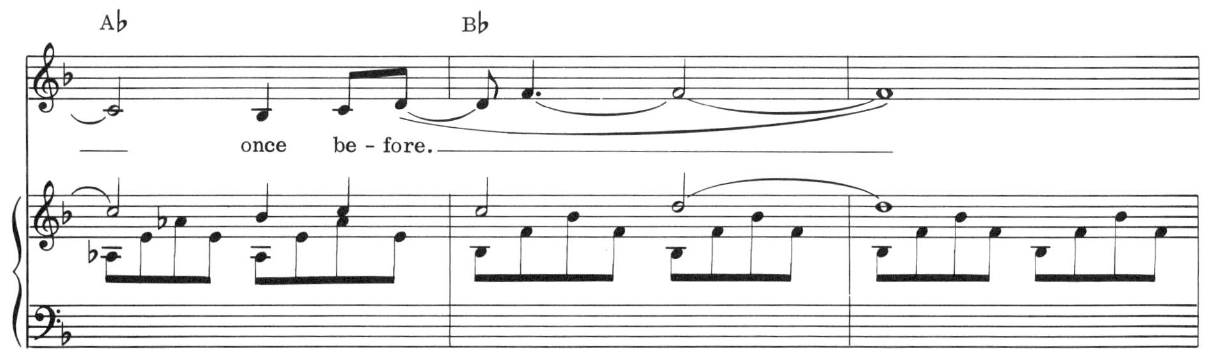

B♭
I'll take the sword and the shield,
'Cause

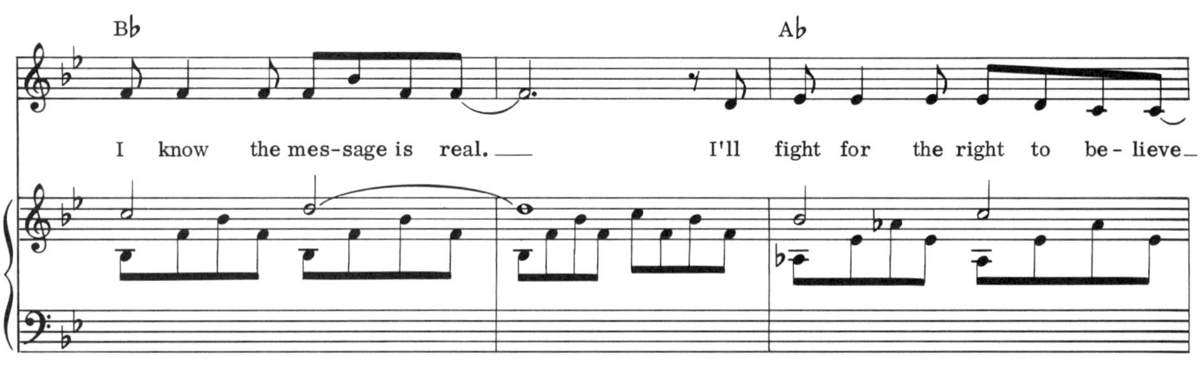
B♭
A♭
I know the mes-sage is real.
I'll fight for the right to be-lieve

A♭
B♭
in His cause.

B♭
I see the bat-tle be-gin
And I know which ar-my will win.
bat-tle has on-ly be-gun
Like the ea-gle who looks at the sun,

B♭
A♭
One side will be in con-trol in the end.
And re-al-iz-es what he can be, and then pre-pares.
B♭
harmony 2nd time only
B♭
When I hear the call I will heed
So fas-ten the ar-mor of truth,
B♭
The or-ders of truth I'll re-ceive,
We'll pre-pare while we're yet in our youth,
And
To
A♭
B♭
fight for the right to be-lieve in His cause.
fol-low the on-ly true God, and be-lieve.

harmony both times
B♭
B♭add 9
Stand for what is right. We're the
ff
Fm7/B♭
E♭
war - ri - ors of light, De - fend - ing truth and hon -
E♭
E♭/C
F
- or in our lives. The
B♭add 9
truth we will be - lieve. We will

Fm7/B♭
fight for vic - to - ry.
E♭
To ⊕
Con - quer the en - e - my with all our
E♭/F
F
B♭
might. Stand for the right.
B♭
A♭
D.S. al Coda
The
D.S. al Coda

Coda
E♭/F
E/F♯
F♯7
might.
B add 9
Stand for what is right. We're the
F♯m7/B
war - ri - ors of light, De -
E
fend - ing truth and hon - or in our

E/F♯
F♯
B add 9
lives. ___
The truth we will ___ be - lieve ___
B add 9
F♯m7/B
We will fight for vic - to - ry. ___
E
Con - quer the en - e - my ___ with all ___ our
E/F♯
F♯
B
might. ___
ff

YOU GAVE ME MORE

Arranged by
Greg Hansen

Words and Music by
AFTERGLOW

Bm7
Bm7/E
A
Asus
Bm7/E
To - geth - er on our way.
A
A/C♯
We could - n't real - ly know
D6
D
D6
Bm7/E
E
We'd have to face this day.
A sus add 9
A
A/C♯
And now the time has come.

Bm7
Bm7/E
A
Asus
Bm7/E
I hope that you can see.
A
A/C#
Bm7
In spite of all the things we've lost,
D6
Bm7/E
How much you've left to me.
And
A
C#m7
Bm7
Bm7/E
you, you gave me more than words could ev - er
you, you taught more than I'll ev - er un - der -

A
C♯m7
Dma7
Bm7/E
say. You gave me hope, — You brushed my tears a -
stand. You lift - ed me, — You led me by the
A
F♯m
D
A/C♯
way. The things that you — have giv - en, Are
hand. You must have just — been with us To
Bm7
A/C♯
1. D
A/C♯
mine to have — and hold; The trea - sures that you shared with me — shine
show a bet - ter way; You
Bm7
Bm7/E
2. Bm7
Bm7/E
To ⊕ (on D.S.)
bright - er now — than gold, And gave me more — than words could ev - er

A
say.

Asus add 9
A
A/C♯
With char - i - ty and peace

Bm7
Bm7/E
A
Asus
Bm7/E
You taught us how to love.

A
A/C♯
Bm7
You've gone be - fore to lead the way,
D6
D
E
Pre - par - ing homes a - bove.
A
A/C♯
And some bright fu - ture day,
Bm7
Bm7/E
A
Asus
Bm7/E
To - geth - er once a - gain,

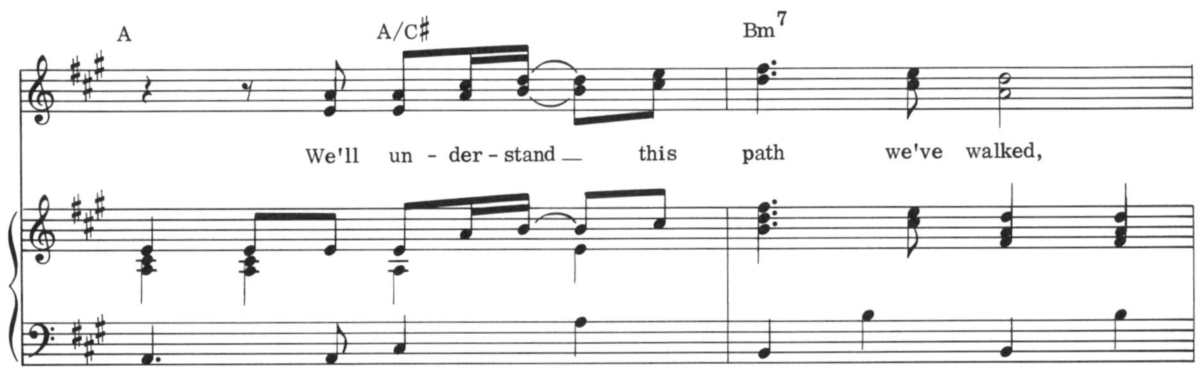
A
A/C♯
Bm7
We'll un - der - stand — this path we've walked,

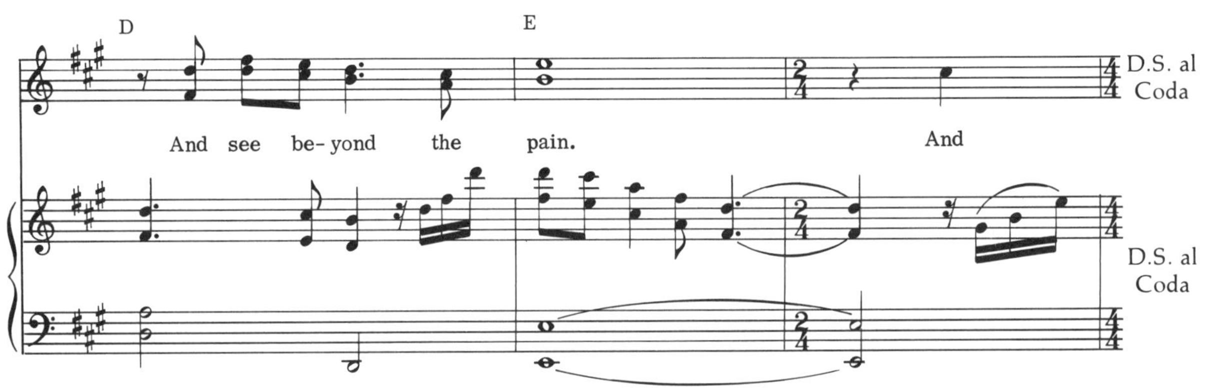
D
E
And see be- yond the pain. And
D.S. al Coda
D.S. al Coda

Coda
A
F♯m
D
Bm7/E
say. You gave me more — than words could ev - er
rit.

A
say.
3
a tempo
rit.
pp

STANDING AS A WITNESS

Arranged by
Greg Hansen

Words and Music by
AFTERGLOW

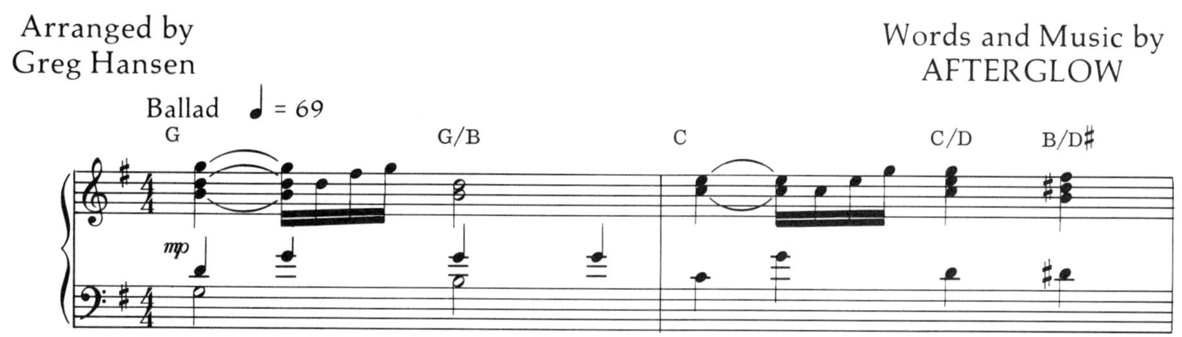

Em
E♭m(♯5)
G/D
A7/C♯
Am7
souls.
land.
Will they ev - er know the way?
Help them un - der - stand the way.
Am7/D
G
G/B
See the light,
Feel the love,
C
C/D
G
G/B
Shin - ing through the dark - ness of our time, And the light,
love that turns the dark - ness in - to day, And the love,
C
C/D
B/D♯
Em
E♭m(♯5)
Show - ing how to reach our home di - vine.
love that we must have to lead the way.

G/D
A7/C#
Am7
Let our light so shine to - day.
Give your love a - way to - day.
Am7/D
G
G/B
Bm7
Bm7/E Em
Stand - ing as a wit - ness,
Hold - ing to the pro - mise.
Am
Am/D
D
G
G/B
Walk - ing in the path - ways that He trod.
Stand - ing as a wit - ness,
Bm7
Bm7/E Em
Am7
Am7/D
1.
G
G/B
With His name up - on us,
Stand - ing as a wit - ness of our God.

C C/D
2.
G D/G E7
A A A/C#
God.
Stand-ing as a wit-ness,
C#m7 C#m7/F# Bm Bm/E E
Hold-ing to the pro-mise. Walk-ing in the path-ways that He trod.
A A/C# C#m7 C#m7/F# Bm7 Bm7/E
Stand-ing as a wit-ness, With His name up-on us. Stand-ing as a wit-ness of our
A A/C# D D/E A
God.

YOU'RE MY FRIEND

Arranged by
Greg Hansen

Words and Music by
AFTERGLOW

Dm7
G7
Learn - ing how to be a friend.
C add 9
Learn - ing how to un - der - stand.
When I
C add 9
Am
stum - ble and fall,
it's you af - ter all
That's
B♭ma7
Dm7
run - ning just as fast as you can,
To

Dm7/G
G7
pick me up and help me to stand, And
C add 9
C9
help me start all o - ver a - gain. You're my
Fma9
Dm7
Dm/G
friend, Help - ing me walk down this
Cma9
Am
Gm/C
C
Fma9
road. And you make it ea - sy, When

Dm
Dm7/G
Cma9
you help me car - ry my load.
Am
Gm7/C
C
Fma9
Dm7
When I need a shoul - der to lean on at times,
Em7
Am7
Rain or shine, you're al - ways there. You're a
B♭ma7
Dm
Dm/G
To
friend who's al - ways help - ing, Hold - ing out your hand to share.

C add 9
G7
C add 9
When - ev - er the storm
Am7
Dm7
Dm7/G
was dark, The rain - bow was right be - hind. You
Dm7
G7
C add 9
helped me to see that this life could be The great - est thing I could find.
Am7
Now I see and un - der - stand That

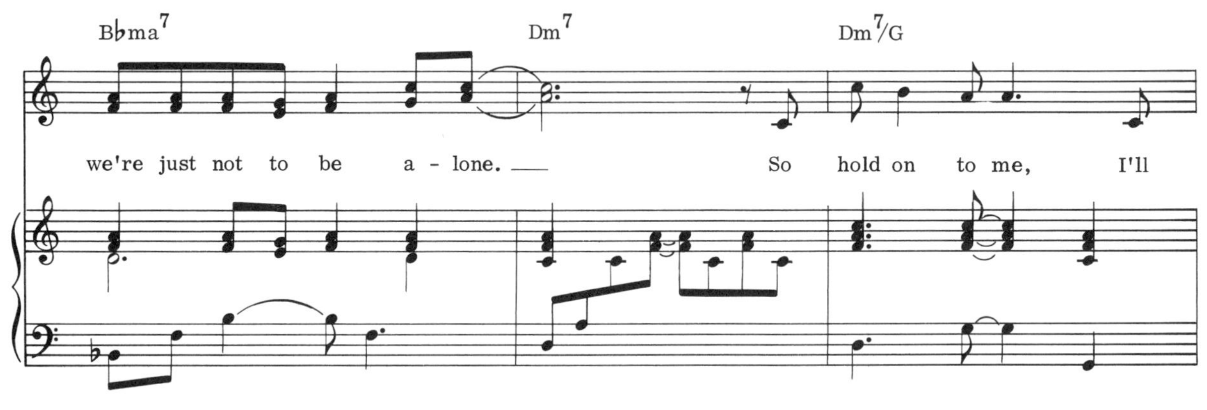
B♭ma7
Dm7
Dm7/G
we're just not to be a - lone. So hold on to me, I'll

G7
C add 9
C9
hold on to you, as we walk this road back home. You're my
D.S. al Coda
D.S. al Coda

Coda
C add 9
F ma7
If ev - er you feel that

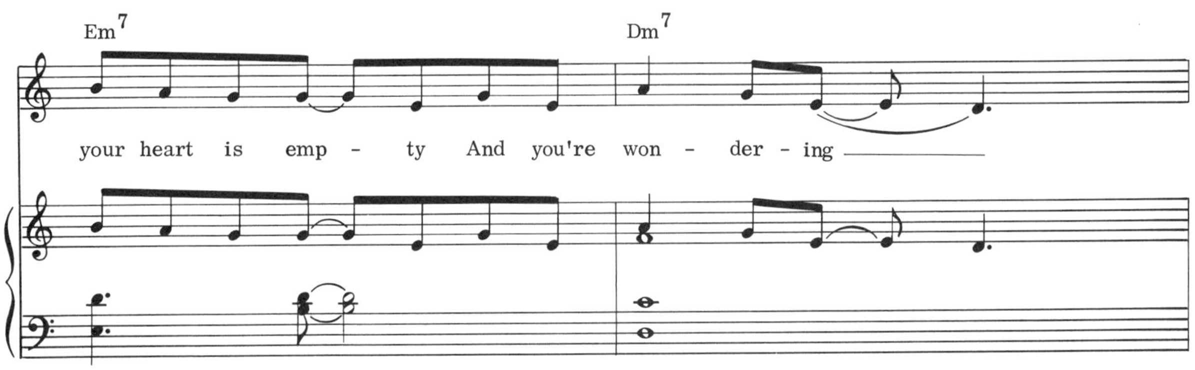
Em7
Dm7
your heart is emp - ty And you're won - der - ing

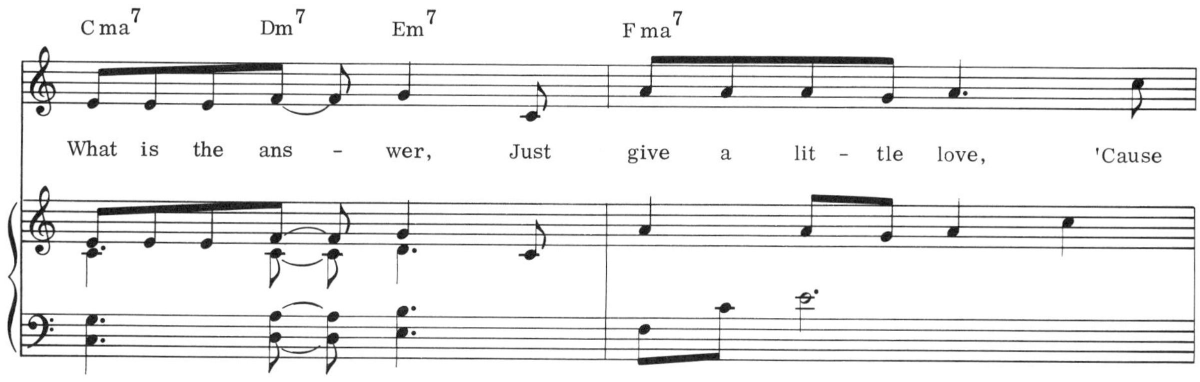
Cma7
Dm7
Em7
Fma7
What is the ans - wer, Just give a lit - tle love, 'Cause

Em7
Dm7
Dm7/G
ev - 'ry - bod - y needs some - one to be - lieve in And hold on

Em7/A
to.
You're my
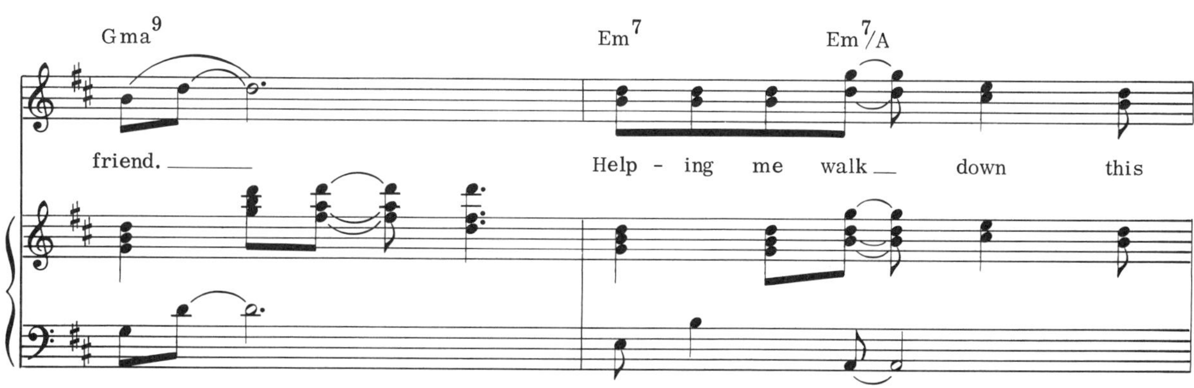
Gma9
Em7
Em7/A
friend.
Help - ing me walk down this

Dma7 Bm Am/D D Gma9
road. And you make it ea - sy, — When
Em Em7/A Dma9
you help me car - ry my load. —
Bm7 Am/D D Gma9 Em7
When I need a shoul - der — to lean on at times —
F♯m7 Bm7 Cma9
Rain or shine, you're al - ways there. — You're a friend who's al - ways help - ing,

Em7
Em7/A
F♯m7
Hold - ing out your hand, A friend who's al - ways help - ing me
Bm7
Em7
Em7/A
to un - der - stand. We're all in need of some - one. Ev - 'ry - bod - y needs a
D add 9
F♯m7
D add 9
Bm7
Em7
friend. We're all in need of some - one,
Em7/A
D
G/D
D
Ev - 'ry - bod - y needs a friend.
rit.

BROTHERS

Arranged by
Greg Hansen

Words and Music by
AFTERGLOW

(Instrumental Solo on D.S.)
B♭
B♭/C
F
E♭/F
C/B♭
B♭
B♭/C
C7
mf
On - ly we — can take our broth-er's hand.
Broth-ers, — from ev-'ry walk — of
Am
Dm7
B♭6
Gm7
C7
F add 9 sus
F
Gm7/F
F7
life and time.
Wan-d'ring lost — in sha-dow and in pain.
B♭
C7
Am7
Dm7
Broth-ers — who need a touch — of light di - vine, To
B♭
Csus
C7
To
help them see the nar - row way a - gain. —
rit.

F add 9
mp
Bb
Gm7
Broth - ers, to - day and yes - ter - day. The
Gm7
C7
F add 9
Sav - ior taught the per - fect way to love. And He
Am
Bb
Gm
showed us, by the life He free - ly gave, How
Bb
Bb/C
F
C7
D.S. al Coda
we must live to earn our broth - er's love.

Coda
F add 9
Gm7
B♭
B♭/C
Broth-ers, pass-ing by us ev-'ry day, Do we reach for them to help them un-der-
F add 9
Gm7
stand? There's no o-ther if we fail to show the way.
B♭
B♭/C
F add 9
dim.
B♭
p
B♭/C
On-ly we can take our broth-er's hand. On-ly you can take your broth-er's
dim.
p
F sus add 9
F add 9
hand.
rit.

LOVE IN OUR HEARTS

Dm7 C/D Bb add 9 Bb/C
think-ing it's the on - ly way. Why can't we find a lit - tle
look-ing at the oth - er side. Then we will find a lit - tle
lit - tle love we all need to give. That's when we'll find that a lit - tle
take 2nd ending on D.S.
1. F C/F F C/F
love ?
2. Gm7
love in our hearts
Gm7/C C7 Fma9 Dm7
We'll make this world a place Where we
Gm7 Gm7/C C7 Fma7
live with each oth - er and get a - long.

Fma7 Gm7 F Gm7 Gm7/C C7
With love in our hearts We'll find a
f
Fma9 Dm7 Gm7
much bet - ter way, by help - ing each oth -
Gm7/C C7 F C/F F C/F To ⊕
- er car - ry on.
Dm7 C/D Dm7 C/D
D.S. al Coda
D.S. al Coda

Coda
B♭add 9
B♭add 9/C
F ma9
This life's a jour - ney And ev - 'ry - one has a part.
Dm7
B♭add 9
B♭/C
Re-mem-ber to fin - ish, And
F ma9
Dm7
Gm7
lis - ten with all your heart, As you're spread-ing the word called
Gm7/C
F
C/F
F
C/F
love a - round. With

Gm7
Gm7/C
C7
love in our hearts We'll make this
Fma 9
Dm7
world a place Where we
Gm7
Gm7/C
C7
live with each oth - er and get a - long.
Fma7
Gm7
F
With

Gm7
Gm7/C
C7
love in our hearts We'll find a
Fma9
Dm7
much better way, By
Gm7
Gm7/C
helping each other carry on.
F
C/F
F
C/F
Dm7
C/D
Love in our hearts

Dm7
C/D
Dm7
C/D
Love in our hearts,
Love in our hearts,
F
C/F
Dm7
C/D
Dm7
C/D
Love in our hearts,
Love in our hearts,
Love in our hearts,
F
C/F
F
C/F
Love in our hearts,
Love in our hearts,
Dm7
C/D
Dm7
C/D
F
Love in our hearts,
Love in our hearts.